The Midnight Ride of Paul Revere

One if by Land, Two if by Sea

Ellen Min

PowerKiDS press™

NEW YORK

Published in 2016 by The Rosen Publishing Group, Inc.
29 East 21st Street, New York, NY 10010

Photo Credits: Cover © Massachusetts Historical Society, Boston, MA, USA/Bridgeman Images; pp. 5, 21 Stock Montage/Archive Photos/Getty Images; pp. 6, 15 Print Collector/Hulton Archive/Getty Images; pp 7, 19 MPI/Archive Photos/Getty Images; p. 8 Hulton Archive/Getty Images; p. 9. Minneapolis Institute of Arts, MN, USA/Gift of James F. and Louise H. Bell/Bridgeman Images; p. 10 Archive Photos/Getty Images; p. 11 Universal History Archive/UIG/Getty Images; p. 13 MPI/Archive Photos/Getty images; p. 17 Louis S. Glanzman/National Geographic Image Collection/Getty Images; p. 20 The Boston Globe/Getty Images

Library of Congress Cataloging-in-Publication Data

Min, Ellen.
The midnight ride of Paul Revere : one if by land, two if by sea / Ellen Min. -- First edition.
     pages cm. -- (Spotlight on American history)
Includes index.
ISBN 978-1-4994-1736-4 (library bound) -- ISBN 978-1-4994-1734-0 (pbk.) -- ISBN 978-1-4994-1733-3 (6-pack)
1. Revere, Paul, 1735-1818--Juvenile literature. 2. Statesmen--Massachusetts--Biography--Juvenile literature. 3. Massachusetts--History--Revolution, 1775-1783--Juvenile literature. 4. Massachusetts--Biography--Juvenile literature. I. Title.
F69.R43M56 2015
973.3'311092--dc23
                              2015018628

Manufactured in the United States of America

CPSIA Compliance Information: Batch #WS15PK: For Further Information contact Rosen Publishing, New York, New York at 1-800-237-9932

CONTENTS

A FAMOUS POEM

Listen my children and you shall hear
Of the midnight ride of Paul Revere

These lines are the beginning of a famous poem by Henry Wadsworth Longfellow. It was written 40 years after Paul Revere's death.

The story of Paul Revere's ride has been retold many times. On the night of April 18, 1775, Revere rode across the Massachusetts countryside warning people that British soldiers were coming. This helped the people of the Massachusetts Bay **Colony** be ready for the Battles of Lexington and Concord. These were the first battles in the **American Revolution**. In this war, the people of what would become the United States won their freedom from Great Britain.

Revere was a real person. His famous ride really happened. This book tells exactly what happened on Revere's heroic ride. It also tells of other American heroes who rode to warn patriots of the coming of the British army.

This dramatic engraving shows Paul Revere as he rides from Boston to Lexington on *April 18, 1775.*

GROWING UP IN BOSTON

Paul Revere was born in Boston, Massachusetts, on January 1, 1735. His father, Apollos Rivoire, came to Boston from France as a boy. He was 13 years old. His parents sent him to Boston to apprentice to a goldsmith. Later Rivoire changed his name to Revere because it was easier for people to say.

This 19th-century engraving shows a view of Boston and the harbor from Bunker Hill.

The painting shown here depicts a battle scene in 1755 during the French and Indian War. American colonists and British soldiers fought side by side against the French. Native Americans helped both sides.

Paul's father was a successful goldsmith. He taught Paul to make things from fine metals. In time, Paul became a successful silversmith. When Paul was 19, his father died. Paul had to wait until he was 21 to take over his father's business.

In 1756, Revere left the family business to fight in the French and Indian War. The French and Indian War lasted from 1754 until 1763. In this war, the British, the French, and the Native American groups that sided with each fought over parts of North America. Paul Revere survived the war. He returned to Boston to run his father's business.

A SILVERSMITH AND AN ENGRAVER

In 1757, Revere married Sarah Orne. They had eight children together. She died in 1773. Later that year, he married Rachel Walker. They had eight children, too! Revere worked hard to support his big family. He had the help of his younger brother, Thomas. Thomas was

John Singleton Copley painted this portrait of Paul Revere. It is the most famous image of the great patriot.

This 1792 tea service is the most complete set known to be made by Paul Revere.

Paul's first apprentice. As a silversmith, Revere made silver spoons, buckles, teapots, and more. He worked with gold, too. He also **engraved** copper plates. These were used to print drawings. Revere even made false teeth and worked as a dentist for a while!

Revere was a trusted member of his community. He joined many community groups. He was on the **committee** that brought in Boston's first streetlights. Revere also became involved in politics.

COLONIAL LIFE

In 1763, the British won the French and Indian War. At that time, Massachusetts, where Revere lived, was one of several British colonies in North America. Colonies are places people have moved to that are still ruled by the leaders of the country from which they came.

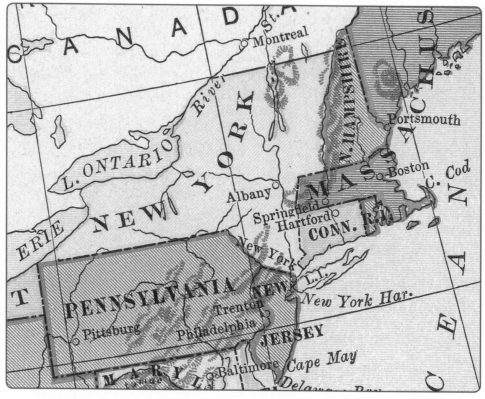

This section of a 1782 map shows Massachusetts and six of the other original 13 states.

The engraving above, from the 1870s, shows angry Bostonians reading the Stamp Act in 1765.

The French and Indian War was expensive. To help pay for it, the British government passed laws that taxed many things colonists bought. For example, the Stamp Act taxed paper goods. The British government also passed laws that put limits on the colonial government. These taxes and laws made many colonists angry. Secret groups called the Sons of Liberty formed to oppose the new laws.

AN EARLY PATRIOT

Historians believe Revere joined the Sons of Liberty, which fought for colonists' rights. He made many engravings to show how patriots felt about unfair British laws. He made an engraving that showed British troops marching off ships into Boston.

On March 5, 1770, British soldiers fired on unarmed Boston civilians. They killed five men. The first man killed was Crispus Attucks, an African American patriot. Paul Revere made an engraving of the event, which came to be called the Boston Massacre.

On December 16, 1773, members of the Sons of Liberty dumped three shiploads of tea into Boston's harbor to protest the British tax on tea. This event became known as the Boston Tea Party. Many believe Paul Revere was among the men who boarded the ships. Later, on December 17, Paul Revere rode to New York and Philadelphia to explain the tea party.

Revere knew that the British soldiers in Boston feared an uprising and planned to capture the colonists' arms and gunpowder. In December 1774, he rode to Portsmouth, New Hampshire, to warn townspeople. The British did not arrive until several days later. When they got there, they discovered the townspeople had captured the fort and taken the supplies!

THE
ASSOCIATION
OF
THE SONS OF LIBERTY,
OF
NEW-YORK.

IT is essential to the Freedom and Security of a Free People, that no Taxes be imposed upon them but by their own Consent, or their Representatives. For " what Property have they, in that, which another may, by Right, take when he pleases, to himself?" The Former is the undoubted Birth-right of *Englishmen*, to secure which, they expended Millions, and sacrificed the Lives of Thousands. And yet, to the Astonishment of all the World, and the Grief of *America*, the Commons of *Great-Britain*, after the Repeal of the memorable and detestable *Stamp Act*, reassumed the Power of imposing Taxes on the *American* Colonies, and insisting on it, as a necessary Badge of Parliamentary Supremacy, passed a Bill, in the seventh Year of his present Majesty's Reign, imposing Duties on all Glass, Painters Colours, Paper, and Teas, that should after the 20th of *November*, 1767, be " imported from *Great-Britain*, into any Colony or Plantation in *America*." This Bill, after the Concurrence of the Lords, obtained the Royal Assent. And thus, they, who from Time immemorial, have exercised the Right of giving to, or withholding from the Crown, their Aids and Subsidies, according to their *own free Will and Pleasure*, signified by their Representatives in Parliament, do, by the Act in Question, deny us, their Brethren in *America*, the Enjoyment of the same Right. As this Denial, and the Execution of that Act, involves our Slavery, and would sap the Foundation of our Freedom, whereby we should become Slaves to our Brethren and Fellow Subjects, born to no greater Stock of Freedom than the *Americans*; the Merchants and Inhabitants of this City, in Conjunction with the Merchants and Inhabitants of the ancient *American* Colonies, entered into an Agreement to decline a Part of their Commerce with *Great-Britain*, until the abovementioned Act should be totally repealed. This Agreement operated so powerfully to the Disadvantage of the Manufacturers of *England*, that many of them were unemployed. To appease their Clamours, and to provide the Subsistence for them, which the Non-Importation Agreement had deprived them of, the Parliament in 1770, repealed so much of the Revenue Act as imposed a Duty on Glass, Painters Colours, and Paper, and left the Duty on Tea, as *a Test of the Parliamentary Right to Tax us*. The Merchants of the Cities of *New-York* and *Philadelphia*, having strictly adhered to the Agreement, so far as it related to the Importation of Articles subject to an *American* Duty; have convinced the Ministry, that some other Measure must be adopted, to execute Parliamentary Supremacy, over this Country; and to remove the Distress brought on the *East India* Company, by the ill Policy of that Act. Accordingly, to increase the Temptation, to the Shippers of Tea from *England*, an Act of Parliament passed the last Session, which gives the whole Duty on Tea, the Company were subject to pay, upon the Importation of it into *England*, to the Purchasers, and Exporters; and when the Company have Ten Millions of Pounds of Tea, in their Warehouses, exclusive of the Quantity they may want to ship, they are allowed to export Tea, discharged from the Payment of that Duty, with which they were before chargeable. In Hopes of Aid in the Execution of this Project, by the Influence of the Owners of the *American* Ships, Application was made, by the Company, to the Captains of those Ships, to take the Tea on Freight; but they virtuously rejected it. Still determined on the Scheme, they have chartered Ships to bring over the Tea to this Country, which may be hourly expected, to make an important Trial of our Virtue. If they succeed in the Sale of that Tea, we shall have no Property that we can call our own, and then we may bid adieu to

dreaded,—
Liberty,
mit to our
bute to t
those imp
of NEW

The Sons of Liberty of New York created the proclamation shown here in 1773. Five resolutions condemn the British tax on tea and the colonials who support it.

following RESOLUTIONS, *Viz.*

1st. RESOLVED, That whoever shall aid, or abet, or in any Manner assist, in the Introduction of Tea, from any Place whatsoever, into this Colony, while it is subject by a *British* Act of Parliament, to the Payment of a

PAUL REVERE'S FAMOUS RIDE

On April 18, 1775, Joseph Warren told Revere that the British were sending soldiers to Lexington to arrest colonial leaders John Hancock and Samuel Adams. Revere was afraid of this. He had made a plan in case he was unable to leave Boston. He had organized a signal system, which patriots would be able to see, from the steeple of the tallest church in Boston. Lanterns would tell the patriots in Charlestown if the British were coming by land or sea. There would be one lantern if by land and two if by sea.

Revere slipped out of Boston by boat. He landed in Charlestown, Massachusetts, and borrowed a horse to ride to Lexington. Along the way, he told people about the soldiers' plans. After reaching Lexington, he headed to Concord, where colonists stored supplies. He was stopped by the British from getting to Concord. Others were able to warn the **militia** there. Revere's warning let Hancock and Adams escape. It also gave colonial militias time to gather. When the British reached Lexington **Common**, fighting broke out. The British pushed through to Concord, but the colonial militia, now 500 men, eventually pushed the British back to Boston.

This engraving shows Paul Revere on April 18, 1775, stopping on his ride from Boston to Lexington. He is warning colonists that the British are coming.

WILLIAM DAWES, SAMUEL PRESCOTT, AND SYBIL LUDINGTON

Revere wasn't the only rider that night. Though Revere got there first, William Dawes also carried the news from Boston to Lexington. On the way to Concord, Revere and Dawes ran into Samuel Prescott. Then, a group of British soldiers captured them. Only Prescott escaped to warn Concord.

Two years after Revere's ride, a less famous but equally courageous ride took place. A 16-year-old girl named Sybil Ludington rode all through the night to warn colonists in four villages of New York that the British were attacking a nearby town. She rode 40 miles (64 kilometers). This was almost twice the distance that Paul Revere had covered.

Ludington rode all night through the dark woods. She faced many dangers. Because of her bravery, nearly an entire colonial regiment was gathered by daybreak to fight the British.

The dramatic illustration above of Sybil Ludington's ride was created in 1975. It celebrates her bravery.

AN OFFICER IN THE MILITIA

Though Revere was captured before reaching Concord, he soon convinced the British to free him. As fighting broke out on Lexington Common, Revere helped move a trunk of important papers from a **tavern** in which the British could have captured it.

After the Battles of Lexington and Concord, Revere carried word of the militia's win to other colonies. This convinced many colonists to join the fight against Britain. Others, known as **Loyalists**, sided with the British.

Revere joined the Massachusetts militia in 1776. In 1779, he took part in the Penobscot Expedition. That summer, 700 British soldiers went to Penobscot Bay, in Maine. Maine was part of Massachusetts then. The British presence there was very dangerous. Paul Revere sailed with the American **navy**. He was in charge of the seven cannons for the attack by land. The attack was the worst defeat for the American navy. Paul Revere was not responsible for this failure. The American navy failed to drive the British from the Penobscot Peninsula.

The *initial assault by the Americans at present-day Castine, Maine, on July 28, 1779, was a success. This illustration shows the British redcoats fleeing.*

AN ENTREPRENEUR AFTER THE WAR

The British surrendered in 1781, ending the fighting. In 1783, the two countries signed a peace **treaty**. Revere returned to his silversmith business. In 1788, he opened a **foundry**, or place where metal is cast. It made cannons, bells, and parts for ships. Paul Revere cast the first bell in Boston in 1792. It weighed almost 1,000 pounds (454 kilograms). He was very proud of his work. Some of his bells are still used today.

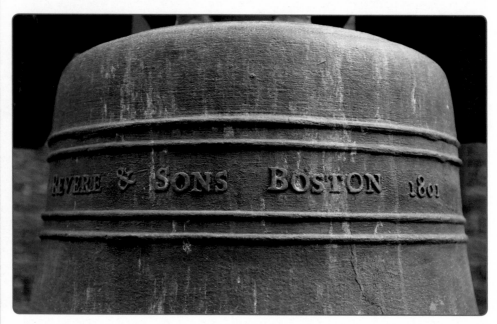

Paul Revere made this 876-pound (397 kg) bell in 1801 for the First Baptist Church of Westborough, Massachusetts.

Paul Revere & Son,

At their BELL and CANNON FOUNDERY, at the North Part of BOSTON,

CAST BELLS, of all fizes; every kind of Brafs ORDNANCE, and every kind of Compofition Work, for SHIPS, &c. at the fhorteft notice:

This newspaper advertisement for the Paul Revere & Son Bell and Cannon Foundry appeared in the early 1800s. It lists many of the items that Paul Revere's company provided.

In 1801, Revere opened the first American copper-rolling mill. He made sheets of copper. This was very important for the American navy. The navy put the copper on the bottoms of its ships. The first ship to receive the copper was the *Constitution*. It had an important role in the War of 1812. All of Paul Revere's hard work made him a rich man. He died in Boston on May 10, 1818, at the age of 83.

PAUL REVERE'S FAME

Paul Revere's fame grew even greater after his death. Henry Wadsworth Longfellow's famous poem, "Paul Revere's Ride," was read by everyone throughout the United States. The poem tells a simple story. The facts were more complicated. Paul Revere was not the only rider who warned the colonists. The poem does not talk about Samuel Prescott or William Dawes. The lanterns in the steeple of the Old North Church were a backup plan in case Paul Revere was caught. The poem, however, creates an energy and excitement that reflects the bravery of this American hero.

The beautiful objects that he created as a silversmith are in museums today. His engravings document key moments in the American Revolution. Paul Revere would have been famous even if he had not made his midnight ride.

GLOSSARY

American Revolution (uh-MER-uh-ken reh-vuh-LOO-shun) Battles that soldiers from the colonies fought against Britain for freedom, from 1775 to 1783.

colony (KAH-luh-nee) A new place where people move that is still ruled by the leaders of the country from which they came.

committee (kuh-MIH-tee) A group of people directed to oversee or consider a matter.

common (KAH-mun) An open area in a town or city not owned by any one person, much like a park today.

engraved (en-GRAYVD) Carved into.

foundry (FOWN-dree) A place where metal is melted and shaped.

Loyalists (LOY-uh-lists) People who were faithful to the British Crown during the American Revolution.

militia (muh-LIH-shu) A group of people who are trained and ready to fight when needed.

navy (NAY-vee) A group of sailors who are trained to fight at sea.

tavern (TA-vurn) A place to spend the night and eat a meal.

treaty (TREE-tee) An official agreement, signed and agreed upon by each party.

INDEX

PRIMARY SOURCE LIST

Page 8: *Paul Revere* by John Singleton Copley (1738–1815). Painted in 1768. Donated by Revere's relatives to the Museum of Fine Arts, Boston.

Page 11: An 1870 engraving of Bostonians reading the Stamp Act, created by an English artist of the 19th century.

Page 13: Image of an original document by the Sons of Liberty, published in 1773.

Page 15: Engraving of Paul Revere talking to John Sullivan was published in *Harper's Encyclopedia of United States History from 458 A.D. to 1905, Volume 10,* by Benson John Lossing and Woodrow Wilson, Harper & Brothers Publishers, New York/London, in 1905.

Page 21: Ad for the Paul Revere & Son Bell and Cannon Foundry, Boston, Massachusetts. The ad appeared in the Boston newspaper called the *Columbian Centinel* on April 3, 1805.

WEBSITES

Due to the changing nature of Internet links, PowerKids Press has developed an online list of websites related to the subject of this book. This site is updated regularly. Please use this link to access the list: www.powerkidslinks.com/soah/paul